walt's pilgrimage jr.

a biographical, photographic storybook of important places in the life of Walt Disney

by

christopher w. tremblay

DEDICATED TO

My godchildren
Karina Bursch
Hannah Reier
Logan Watts

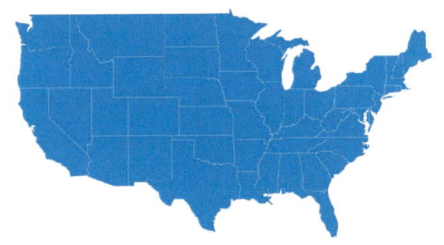

Join us as we travel through the life of Walt Disney!

On this adventure, we will visit the states of Illinois, Missouri, California, and Michigan.

TABLE OF CONTENTS

About Walt Disney..5

Chicago, Illinois..6-9

Marceline, Missouri..10-15

Kansas City, Missouri..16-18

Los Angeles, California..19

Anaheim, California...20

Burbank, California..21

Hollywood, California..22

Hickory Corners, Michigan..23

Mineral King, California...24

Glendale, California..25

San Francisco, California...27

Los Angeles, California..28

Disneyland..29

About Walt Disney

Walter Elias Disney was born December 5, 1901 in Chicago, Illinois. He co-founded The Walt Disney Company, with his brother Roy in 1923. He is most known for the creation of Mickey Mouse.

Walt grew up in Chicago (IL), Marceline (MO) and Kansas City (MO) before moving to California.

Walt was married to Lillian Bounds and they had two children: Diane and Sharon Disney.

Walt is the recipient of 22 Academy Awards for his films and created Disneyland and Walt Disney World.

He died on December 15, 1966 and is buried in Glendale, California.

CHICAGO

Walter Elias Disney was born in Chicago in the Hermosa Neighborhood on Tripp Avenue, which is now called Honorary Disney Family Avenue.

Walt's mother, Flora, designed the house. Walt's father, Elias, built the house.

Walt and his 3 brothers and 1 sister lived here until 1906, when they moved to Marceline, Missouri.

CHICAGO

This is the neighborhood church where Walt Disney was baptized.

His father helped build the church.

CHICAGO

Walt attended McKinley High School in Chicago for one year only. While he was a student here, he drew for the student newspaper, *The Voice*.

CHICAGO

As a child, Walt played in a field near this barn in Marceline and by The Dreaming Tree.

MARCELINE

This was the Disney home where Walt lived during his time in Marceline.

MARCELINE

Now the old train depot in Marceline is home to the Walt Disney Hometown Museum.

**The town even named
the elementary school after him.**

MARCELINE

**Walt was the Chair of the 1966 Winter Olympic Games.
He donated one of the flag poles to
Walt Disney Elementary School in Marceline.**

MARCELINE

MARCELINE

A special Walt Disney tribute stamp was issued in 1968 and in 2003, the Marceline post office was renamed the Walt Disney Post Office.

**3028 Bellafontaine:
One of the homes in Kansas City where
Walt lived with his family.**

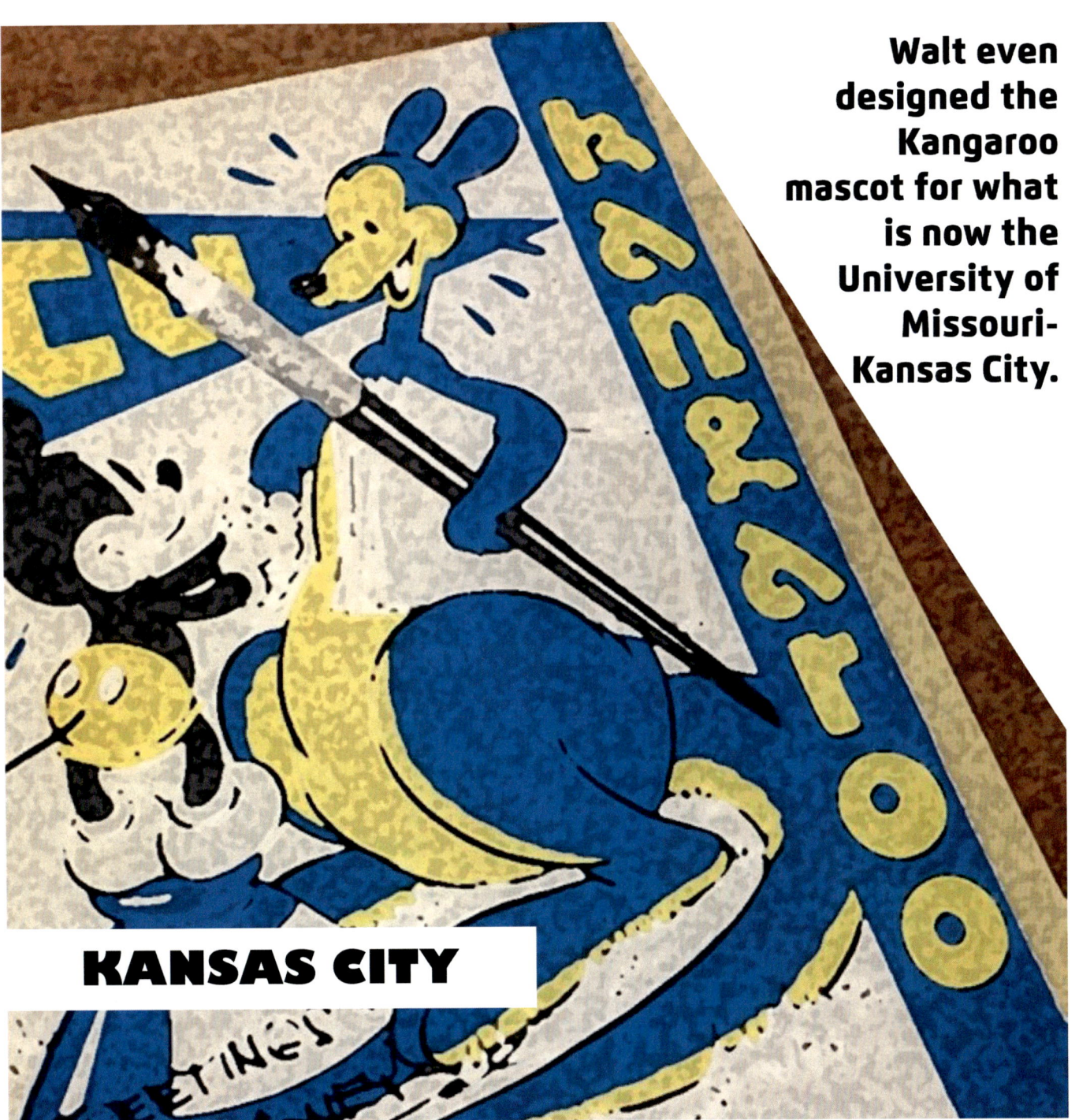

Walt even designed the Kangaroo mascot for what is now the University of Missouri-Kansas City.

KANSAS CITY

This is the site of Laugh-O-gram Films, Inc., a business established by Walt. But unfortunately, it did not last long.

He then moved to California.

The Griffith Park Merry-Go-Round is where
Walt would take his daughters to ride.
This was part of the inspiration for Disneyland.

LOS ANGELES

Walt designed Disneyland, which opened in 1955.

It is home to Sleeping Beauty Castle.

ANAHEIM

BURBANK

**Walt's 1966 Office in the 3H Wing
at The Walt Disney Studios in Burbank, California.**

HOLLYWOOD

Walt has two stars in the Hollywood Walk of Fame in California. One star is for his work in film and the other star is for his work in television.

At the Gilmore Car Museum in Hickory Corners, Michigan, you can see a life-size set piece from the movie, *The Gnome-Mobile*. Walt Disney was friends with Donald Gilmore, who founded the car museum.

MICHIGAN

Walt Disney almost built a ski resort in Mineral King, which is now a part of the Sequoia National Park in California.

MINERAL KING

GLENDALE

Walt Disney died on December 15, 1966. He is buried at the Forest Lawn Cemetery in Glendale, California with other family members.

After Walt Disney died, many buildings were created and named for him — to honor him and his impact in our world.

The next couple of pages are examples of two places in California that honor Walt Disney.

SAN FRANCISCO

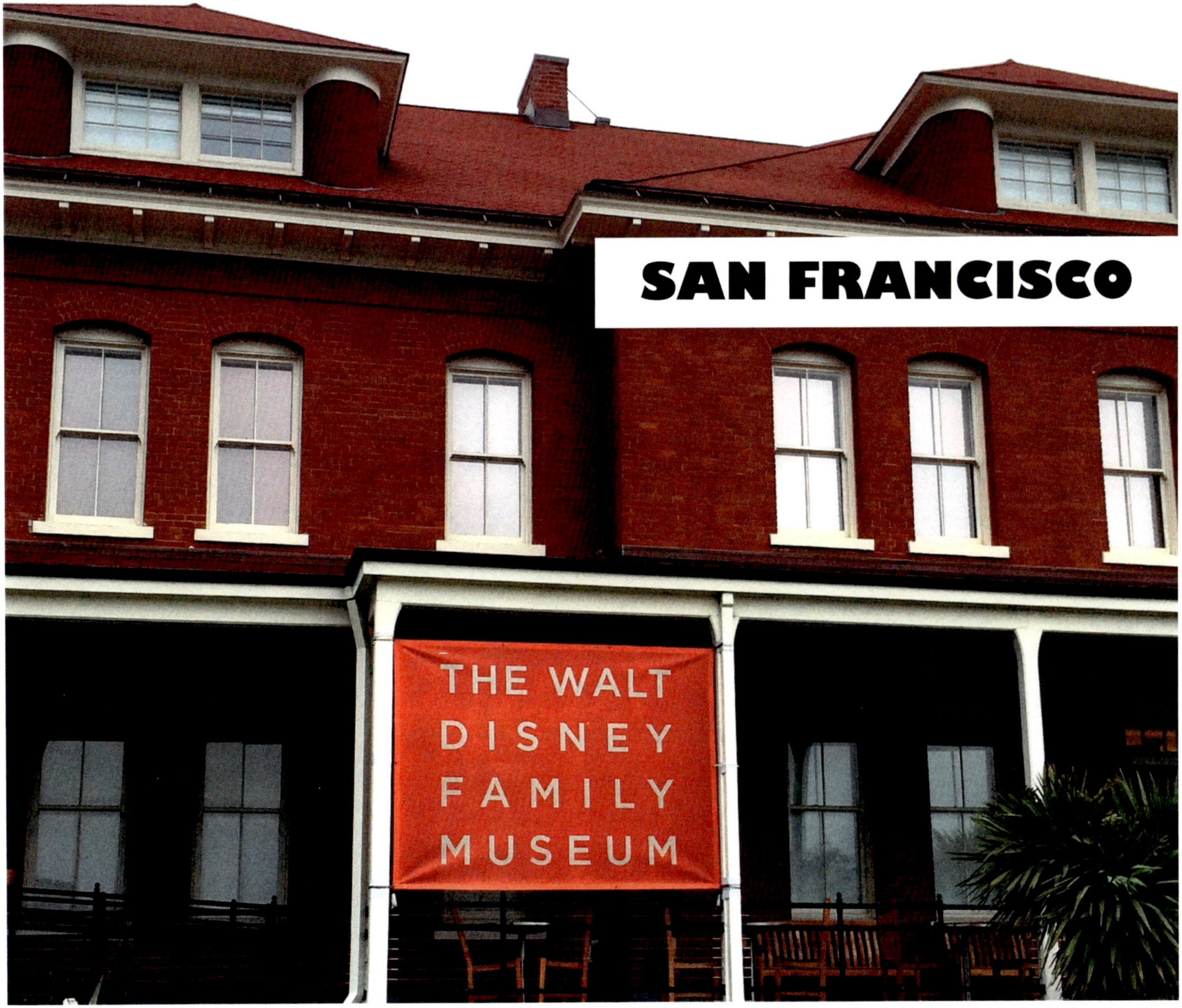

One of Walt's daughters, Diane Disney Miller, created this museum in 2003 in San Francisco to honor her father.

LOS ANGELES

The Walt Disney Concert Hall in downtown Los Angeles, California, is dedicated to Walt Disney. It was made possible by Walt's wife, Lillian.

This "Partners Statue" of Walt with Mickey Mouse reminds us that it all started with a mouse...

DISNEYLAND

Are you the next Walt Disney?

QUESTIONS

What did you learn about Walt Disney?

What place in Walt Disney's life interested you the most and why?

Have you ever visited any of these cities or states?

What place in Walt Disney's life would you like to visit with your family or friends?

Where did you and your family (parents, grandparents, aunts, uncles, cousins) grow up?

If you created a book like this one with pictures of places in your childhood, what places would you include and why?

ABOUT THE AUTHOR

Dr. Christopher W. Tremblay is a Disney historian, researcher, and scholar — and has been fascinated by Disney since his parents took him to Walt Disney World when he was 5 years old (see photo to the right). During his undergraduate studies, Tremblay participated in the Walt Disney World College Program (WDWCP) in 1993, where he spent a semester learning all about the Disney enterprise and earned his "Ducktorate Degree" and the Rachel Imilio Scholarship for designing a new theme park called "Downtown Disney." That is also when he received his first set of mouse ears. In 2015, Dr. Tremblay developed and first taught "Walt's Pilgrimage," a course in the Study in the States Program for students enrolled in the Lee Honors College at Western Michigan University. He is a member of the Disney Alumni Association and a shareholder of The Walt Disney Company. Tremblay has supported The Walt Disney Birthplace and has a brick at the Walt Disney Hometown Museum and in front of the Magic Kingdom at Walt Disney World's "Walk Around the World." He earned his Doctor of Education degree from the University of Michigan-Dearborn. He is also the author of *Walt's Pilgrimage: A Journey in the Life of Walter Elias Disney*. This is Tremblay's second children's book. He co-authored *Lucy's Laptop* (A part of the Creative Character Series) with Sr. Dorothy K. Ederer in 2017. Contact Tremblay at waltspilgrimage@gmail.com.

waltspilgrimage.com

SPECIAL THANKS

Thank you to Carrie Davies of North Oakview Elementary School in Grand Rapids, Michigan, for sharing her expertise in the production of this book.

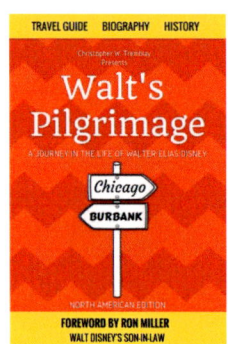

For the youth and adult version of this book, check out *Walt's Pilgrimage.*

All photos taken were taken by Christopher W. Tremblay

Made in the USA
Columbia, SC
25 October 2018